How to Get Started in Free-Machine Embroidery

An inspirational guide with **5 projects** and techniques to feed your creativity

Margo Price

Publishing and Legal Notices

Copyright

Liability

We have used our best efforts to ensure that the content of this document is both useful and correct at the time of publication. The content of this document is supplied for information only and is subject to change without notice. The authors assume no responsibility or liability for any errors or inaccuracies that may appear in this document, nor the use to which it may be put.

This document is for information only and does not represent a legal contract or agreement.

Publishing Information

Author:	Margo Price
	www.time4me-workshops.co.uk
Editor/Designer:	Andrew A Moore
Published By:	AAM Design Limited
	www.aamdesign.co.uk
Publication Number:	T4M-003
Issue Number:	1
Issue Date:	December 2013

About this Document

This document is based on the business model developed and used by Margo Price for running Time4me Workshops. This document describes how to set up and run a home-based craft business, using machine sewing as an example throughout.

Contents

Part 1: Introduction

Exploring the items you'll need for free-machine embroidery.

Welcome

I have been sewing for over thirty years and teaching sewing machine skills for over twelve. In that time I have tried, and become skilled at, a number of different types of sewing.

About Margo Price

My first love was dressmaking, then, once I saw the infinite possibilities of patchwork and quilting, I switched my allegiance. A spell in soft toymaking was soon to follow but not to last. Then I discovered the absolute delights of free-machine embroidery and here I have stayed.

I should explain that when I talk about free-machine embroidery, in this book, I mean the sort of embroidery performed with a darning or embroidery foot fitted, the feed dogs dropped out of action and the top tension reduced to between 0 and 1. I am not talking about embroidery using the pre-programmed fancy stitches provided on most mid-level sewing machines or the pre-programmed digital images which can be stitched out by specialist embroidery machines. Free-machine embroidery is the most basic type of machine embroidery. It requires the minimum of equipment, the minimum of financial outlay and, as far as I am concerned, is the most creative and exciting type of embroidery of all.

Free-machine embroidery has been my passion for many years and I've always been fascinated by just how much you can do with so little equipment. All you need to get started in this wonderful art is a basic sewing machine, a hoop, some fabric, thread and a bit of patience to get used to the technique.

What's in this Book?

This book attempts to give you an overview of what you can do in free-machine embroidery. It is a huge subject and its many followers and practitioners are discovering new and different ways to do things every day. You can:

- Add appliqué designs.
- Write words or messages in thread.
- Decorate large items with free-motion quilting.
- Create pictures – outlined or filled in.
- Make jewellery and decorative pieces using dissolvable fabrics.
- Design three-dimensional pieces.

Using free-machine embroidery, you can stitch in any direction, you can go over the same area repeatedly, you can build up depth, mix colours, and create shading. Really, the possibilities are endless.

If, once you have tried all the projects I have suggested in this book, you decide you want to delve into one particular aspect even deeper; there are numerous books that will help you on your way. See the reading list at the end of this book for more ideas.

You might not want to follow all of the ideas I've given you here and what you choose to do may depend on your particular machine, skill and level of confidence. It may also depend on whether you want to concentrate on the artistic side of Free-machine embroidery or use it for more practical projects. The choice is yours.

Free-machine embroidery really is very freeing once you get the hang of it. The ability to do continuous stitching without having to worry about changing feet or stitch length is really just like drawing with a needle.

So whatever else you get out of this book, make sure you have fun!

If you find this book useful and inspiring please leave me a review at www.Amazon.com or www.Amazon.co.uk and let me know, either through my website, www.time4me-workshops.co.uk, or my facebook page www.facebook.com/pages/Margo-Price-Author . Similarly, if you have any questions or problems then I'd like to hear about that too.

Will Any Sewing Machine Do?

Is your sewing machine capable of free-machine embroidery? In this section we will look at the features and functions you will need to get started.

Basic is Best

I may be accused of being old fashioned, but, when it comes to sewing machines for free-machine embroidery; I have to say that basic is best.

I can speak from experience as I have had a wide range of sewing machines, from the top-of-the-range all-singing-all-dancing, embroidery machine, to the very basic hand-cranked Singer.

The embroidery machine was capable of free-machine embroidery but changing tension was a battle of wills and the least little infraction was greeted with a stall and multi-coloured warning message. The little hand-cranked Singer was willing and able, but two hands are definitely better than one when it comes to free-machine embroidery.

I now have a base model Bernina which is a sturdy, uncomplicated workhorse and does everything I need.

Characteristics of a Good Basic Machine

Machines that are going to be best for free-machine embroidery need to be quite weighty models. You're going to be doing a lot of fast sewing and it's going to be taking a bit of a hammering, so it needs to be quite stable. Unfortunately, this means that a lot of lightweight budget models are not really up to the job.

It would be easy for me to say that any basic sewing machine would be fine for free-machine embroidery – but that wouldn't be true and, as I want you to get the most out of this book, and your introduction to Free-machine embroidery, I want to be honest with you – right from the start.

In my opinion, sewing machines which have a vertically-loaded bobbin and are strongly built, with a metal frame, are best for free-machine embroidery. It is no coincidence that so many well-known Free-machine embroiderers swear by older or industrial-style machines for their work. There are also many people who prefer the original Singer treadle machines for their embroidery. I have one myself, but I am thinking about getting it converted to electricity. Its curren mode of operation may be a great workout for th legs, but starting and stopping takes quite a bit of practice.

Bobbins

Horizontal (Drop-In) and Vertical Bobbins

The most important thing to consider when it comes to bobbins is the bobbin case.

Machines with vertically loaded bobbins have removable bobbin cases and this is best for free-machine embroidery.

If you can get a machine with a vertically-mounted removable case, it will make your life so much easier when it comes to free-machine embroidery.

It's important to have adjustable bobbin tension as well. On a removable bobbin case, this is done by a single screw on the side of the case.

It's very easy to adjust but never adjust it by more than a quarter of a turn at a time or you will end up over-tightening or losing the screw. With fixed, drop in bobbin cases, the bobbin case has to come out and there are two screws to adjust.

I've tried this on several of my customers' machines and found it quite a pain. So, if you have a choice, go for the vertically loaded bobbin option.

Types of Bobbin Spool

Different types of machine take different types of bobbin spool. Usually, the drop-in type takes plastic spools.

There is absolutely nothing wrong with these although they are obviously not as strong as the metal ones. Recently several base model machines have come onto the market with plastic, drop in bobbin facility and these are adequate for starting off in free-machine embroidery. Ultimately, it is up to you to try several machines for their free-machine embroidery capabilities and buy the one that suits your needs the best.

My old Bernina uses metal bobbins. I like these for their durability and ease of winding, but that's just personal choice.

9

Getting Wound Up

The thing about bobbins is that they must be correctly wound. A bobbin that is not correctly wound will cause you no end of problems. So how can you tell whether it's wound correctly?

First of all you will have read your sewing machine instruction manual to make sure that you've threaded it right for bobbin winding. You must wind enough thread onto the bobbin; too little and the wind will be too loose causing slippage on the reel and a poor stitch construction, too much and the bobbin will not run freely in the case causing tension problems.

So how do you know its wound properly? The depth of the thread should be even from the top to the bottom of the bobbin and not bunched up at either extremity. There should be no ends or loops of threads poking out and it should look completely smooth. If that's the way yours looks, you're doing it right.

Correctly Wound Bobbin

Incorrectly Wound Bobbin

If your bobbin doesn't look quite right, don't just tell yourself 'It'll be ok', because it won't. You'll suffer thread breakages, you'll risk a bird's nest of threads under your needle plate and it will all be a pain and may put you off before you've ever got started. It really is worth getting this bit right.

The other really important thing is, and this causes a myriad of problems, is bobbin threading. Now in most drop-in bobbin machines the threading is similar, it's easy to do and there are even a few little arrows to help you. Some even cut the thread off for you and automatically bring it to the top of the needle bed when you start sewing. But you must make sure that the bobbin is in the right way round or there will be no tension on the bobbin thread. This may cause poor stitch construction and thread or even needle breakage. Take time to check.

The same is true of vertically mounted bobbins, they must be properly threaded. There are no arrows to help you here but it will all be in your instruction manual. Please take time to check.

On a final note, if you have one of the bobbin cases that has a separate little lug for free-machine embroidery, please use it, despite its small and insignificant appearance, it will make a huge difference to your bobbin tension.

Stitches

As far as I'm concerned, when we're talking about free-machine embroidery, stitches fall into two categories, what you need and what would be nice to have. Really, all you need, and all I ever use, is straight stitch. Without the risk of sounding too romantic, with a good well-formed straight stitch you can do virtually anything in free-machine embroidery.

Straight stitch is also very useful for filling in areas of work, shading, if you're doing a pictorial piece, outlining buildings and other objects, writing, either in block letters or copperplate, handwriting style or free-motion quilting.

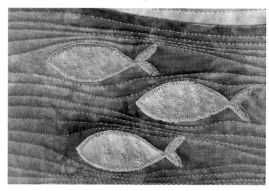

Some people like to use zig-zag stitch. There is no doubt that zig-zag is useful for filling in large areas, particularly when using dissolvable fabrics, when everything needs to be linked together. Most of the modern basic machines can

do zig-zag so, if that's what you've got, you're ok. If you're of the old Singer machine persuasion, you will be stuck with straight stitch, but I can assure you that once you get started, you will soon find that's all you need.

Some people like to include buttonholes in their machine embroidery, either as decoration or to include a fastening in amongst free embroidered work. Most modern machines have a simple one step buttonhole facility and if this appeals to you, give it a try.

Presser Feet

Now presser feet are a bit of a hot potato when it comes to free-machine embroidery. There are those who like to embroider with no foot at all, just using a bare needle. But some experience of what has happened in my classes in the past has led me to believe that this is just too dangerous. It's so easy to get too close to the needle, all it takes is a little distraction and the needle is through your finger. And as I can tell you from experience, that's quite painful. So I always use a darning or embroidery foot, even on my old Singer treadle which, with its standard presser foot shank, will accept a standard modern darning foot. It's safer, goes some way to keeping your fingers away from the needle and affords some support to your fabric. So I would recommend that you always use a presser foot.

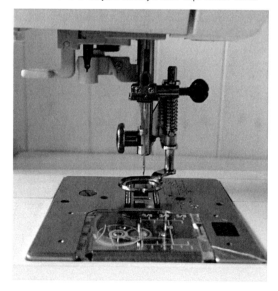

Generic Embroidery Foot on a Standard Shank

There are several different types of embroidery or darning feet and your particular machine may require a particular type. It may even come already supplied with one. But there are several generic models which are more than adequate for the job, unless of course, like me you have a Bernina, which have a completely unique way of attaching presser feet and require the precise model.

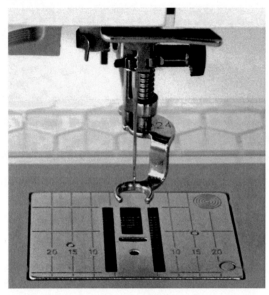

Bernina Embroidery Foot

So before you buy a foot for your embroidery, check the make and model of the machine and the type of shank (the bit the foot screws or clamps onto) and pay a visit to your local sewing machine dealer. They are also widely available online and if you know what you're looking for, you'll probably find it on one of the auction sites or a specialist machine site.

Tension

In free-machine embroidery, tension is everything. There are two main types of tension setting: sewing tension and bobbin tension.

Standard sewing tension is used when you're sewing seams or using one of the programmed embroidery stitches. The ideal tension can vary by a small amount, depending on the machine, and the likely range of settings is marked on the tension knob of most machines. On some computerised machines, the tension is set automatically when the machine is turned on. But when you are doing free-machine embroidery, with the feed dogs dropped out of use, the top tension is normally turned back to zero, or very close to it. This allows the thread to flow faster and freer.

Bobbin tension, depending on the model of machine you have, can be adjusted to allow all sorts of special effects. The effects which can be achieved by adjusting tension in free-machine embroidery can, and do, fill a few books on their own. So if this is an aspect you are particularly interested in, please see the further reading recommendations at the end of this book.

Comfortable Sewing

Now this might seem like an odd topic to include in a sewing manual but I think being comfortable at the sewing machine while you're free embroidering is one of the most important things of all. If you're constantly trying to get a crick out of your neck or thinking about your sore back or you're just not sitting in the right position, then it's going to affect your work. You're not going to put the concentration in that the piece requires – and it will show.

Sit Comfortably

How's your chair? How's its height? Any old dining room or kitchen chair is not going to suitable. I use a secretary-type office chair without arms. Now arms are nice if you want to sit back but they do get in the way. So I've taken the arms off mine, adjusted its height so when I'm sitting at the machine with my arms bent at 90 degrees, my hands rest lightly on the needle bed

You need padding as well. Sitting on a standard wooden chair for hours at a time is going to take its toll on your posterior.

Angle Your Machine

Another thing that's really important is the angle of your sewing machine. When you've been sitting at the sewing machine for any length of time – particularly when you're doing free-machine embroidery, you'll find that your back and neck begin to ache. So what I do is get a hardback book, A4 size and about ½" thick, and wedge it under the back of the sewing machine. Position it so the machine's not rocking around and you will find that this will prevent you leaning forward so much and make your sewing position much more comfortable.

Jacking-up Your Sewing Machine

This is not going to work if you use one of those large, Perspex quilting tables that fit around the arm of your machine and support your work. I personally prefer the standard slide-on table that comes with many machines and allows me to adjust the angle of my machine as much as I want. So give this a try. It looks a bit odd but once you've tried it and felt the benefits, you'll want to do it every time you embroider.

Take a Break...

If you work on a computer regularly, as I do, you are supposed to take regular breaks. This is also true when doing free-machine embroidery. Concentrating on a needle, which is constantly flying up and down, takes its toll very quickly. So you need to schedule regular breaks. When working at the computer, I use an egg-timer, set to 25 minutes, to remind me when it's time to take

a 5 minute break. Now whether you would hear an egg-timer over the clatter of a sewing machine is debateable, but do try and find some way of timing your sewing sessions and reminding yourself to take a break. You'll return to the task refreshed.

...And Stretch

When you take a break, don't just stay sitting at the machine, get up and walk around, do a bit of stretching. Try a few easy yoga poses. I'm not an expert on yoga but I have taken it up recently, by downloading an app to my iPad, and it makes me feel so much better - particularly after a long session of free-machine embroidery. When I'm stitching, I always try to have my yoga mat spread out next to me so I can get up, when the timer rings, and do a few poses. So do give it a try. It will enable you to sew for longer periods without getting stiff and sore.

Look After Your Eyes

By the time we get into our early 50s, as I have, most of us are wearing some form of spectacles. Your eyes naturally get a bit weaker as you age and most of us need help for close work on the sewing machine or computer. Be aware of tiredness as well. If you're eyes start to get tired or feel a bit gritty, stop. You don't want an accident. That would be a real setback, knock your confidence, blood all over your project. So don't risk it. If you feel tired have a break.

The other thing to think about is, are you wearing the right glasses? When did you last have your eyes tested? If it's been a few years and you find you're getting tired quicker than you used to, why not visit your optician?

There is also another safety benefit to wearing glasses, apart from the obvious, and those of you who don't yet need glasses may also like to consider this. If you're embroidering and you hit a pin or a heavily stitched part of your work and the needle breaks and flies upwards, there is every chance it may go in your eye. It's not yet happened to me but I have seen it happen to others and it can be pretty nasty. So, even if you

13

don't need them to see what you're doing, you may like to consider wearing some form of eyewear to protect your eyes. Safety goggles are not really suitable for this but you can buy mild reading glasses from supermarkets and chemists which are ideal. Try and avoid the 'sit on the nose' type of granny glasses as the lenses are usually too narrow to give you much protection.

Apply Good Lighting

Many modern machines, if that's what you're using, do have LED format lighting which provides a more even light and doesn't cast shadows. The more you pay for your machine, more LEDs you get. I had a super-duper embroidery machine for a while, until I realised I wasn't really using all it's features, and it had 12 LEDs! But even with that level of brilliance, I still found that, when doing free-machine embroidery, (as opposed to programmed embroidery) I needed some form of task lighting. I use one of those adjustable 20 Watt halogen lamps – a fiver from your local DIY depot. If you want to spend a bit more and get one with a bendy neck, you can adjust these to focus on the particular area you're working on. If you've got a lamp that you can get a daylight bulb for, then so much the better. Things always look clearer in daylight. I haven't tried this but can appreciate the benefits of it. So if you've taken all the measures I've suggested and are still having trouble seeing what you're doing, try a daylight bulb.

What Threads Should I Use?

The one rule for threads in free-machine embroidery, or any other sewing project for that matter, is make sure it's good. Poor, cheap or inappropriate threads will only undermine all your hard work.

The Importance of Good Thread

Thread is very important. It's particularly important in free-machine embroidery. When you're moving that fast, and once you get the hang of it you will be going pretty fast, the thread will reeling out very quickly and the least little problem with the thread, is going to cause it to break. And that's a real pain. So if you're going to buy thread for machine embroidery, make sure it's the best you can afford.

What Not to Use

Your Sewing Box Inheritance

Lots of us have been left sewing boxes by aunties or grandmas. We have become known as the stitcher in the family and they very kindly leave us their sewing box. It's usually quite old, lots of reels of threads, bits and pieces, some useful, some not so. The trouble is with old threads is they tend to become flattened on the reel and, if you use them on your machine, they're not going to run very smoothly. The quality is not going to match that of modern threads and they are likely to snap. So I would suggest that you keep these old threads for hand sewing. As you can imagine, I've upset a few people by telling them this. Being left something as personal as a sewing box can be very meaningful and hold lots of memories but, unlike antique furniture, wine and paintings, thread does not improve with age. So be kind to yourself and your machine and use a good modern thread.

Threads from Auction Sites

You've probably been on some popular auction sites and seen machine embroidery 'silk' from Thailand or somewhere in the Far East. It's usually very cheap. But there's a reason for that. I've tried them myself, from several different vendors, but at anything other than a snail's pace, they snap, shred and leave you thoroughly fed up. It's really not worth it, save yourself the pain and get something decent.

Bargain Basement

Buying bargain threads from markets, car boot sales, the post office (unless it is also a haberdashery as my local one is) or the corner shop is also a potential road to disaster. Remember at all times, they're cheap for a reason. And the way to tell if a thread is really no good is to unwind a short length from the reel, hold it up to the light and, if it's a bit fluffy or hairy, reject it as that fluff is going to clog up your needle and ultimately, your machine.

Types of Threads

Threads are gauged generally by their thickness. Some manufacturers (I use Madeira but there are many other good brands) indicate thickness by numbers. The higher the number - the thinner the thread. The profile of the thread is also important. Now the profile of a thread can be seen if you snip a bit off the end and look at the thread end on. Standard all purpose polyester threads have a round profile. They generally have a have a dull appearance, on the reel, as when light hits them it is scattered in all directions and very little is reflected back to your eye. Rayon machine embroidery thread has a flat profile and so reflects a lot of light back to your eye, making it look shiny.

Obviously even the best threads will shred or snap occasionally but you can lessen the chances of that happening by buying something good.

So What Threads Do I Recommend?

All I ever use is three types:

- a standard all purpose polyester for general sewing and for bobbin filling when machine embroidering.

- a good quality rayon thread for embroidery.

- a 100% cotton quilting thread for embroidering on quilts and throws.

What Needles Will I Need?

Be sharp about needles. Change your needle often; with each new project, or more frequently if you have accidents, to ensure that your machine is capable of delivering perfect stitches every time.

The Importance of Good Needles

You need to be sharp about your needles. Sorry about the pun, but whatever you do about needles, change them frequently. Over the past ten years, a large number of people have come to me with sewing machines, that are years old, saying they don't sew properly. They complain that the stitches don't look right, the thread breaks, and the fabric gets bunched up. I often discover that they have never changed the needle. So that is the first thing that I suggest they try. It usually makes a world of difference.

So often should you change your needle? I would say after every project or even sooner if you've inadvertently hit a pin when sewing. Obviously, we all forget. We're so excited about getting on to the next project that we're already thinking about which fabric and threads we're going to buy.

But just take a minute to consider your needle. Your sewing will be all the better for it. If your machine's been in storage for a while, in the loft or the wardrobe, if you've been on an extended holiday and your machine's been left out. Just do it a kindness and change the needle. Machine needles are not expensive in proportion to the difference they will make to your sewing.

What Type of Needle to Use

So the needle's been in there for as long as you can remember and you've forgotten what type it was. So what do you replace it with?

There are many types of needle and lots have been written about what you should use for what. For free-machine embroidery, I use a standard embroidery needle, size 12, most of the time. If the fabric I'm using is a little thicker than normal, I may go up to a 14. If it's really thick, i might even stretch to a 16. But when I'm stitching my standard free-machine embroidery appliqué sandwich of two layers of standard mercerized cotton, a layer of batting and a layer of cheap backing fabric, a size12 does the job.

When you get a pack of embroidery needles, do try and buy a good brand. But be aware, however good the brand (it does tend to be fewer the better the brand) there are always going to be at least one or two duds in the pack. That is, they may have burrs, tiny bits of metal left over from the manufacturing process, around the eye or on the shaft. These, as soon as you start to use them, will break or shred your thread.

The eyes of machine needles can be difficult to see, especially a size 12, but if you hold one up to a lamp or look it through a magnifying glass, you may be able to see if there are any small imperfections of sticking out bits. If there are, don't risk using it, just throw it out. While you are looking for burrs, also check that the shaft of the needle is straight. Any bending, however slight can cause real problems as it may not line up with the hole in the needle plate and break as soon as you start to sew. It may also catch on the bobbin case and cause some damage.

If you are doing pictorial embroidery and using heavy canvas or twill as a base, you may find it beneficial to use a Jeans or denim needle. These are very sharp as they are intended to part the fibres of the heavy fabric without breaking them. So if you find that a standard embroidery needle is not man enough for the job, try a denim needle.

Another thing you will need to be aware of once you start free-machine embroidery is that the needle or its shaft may become clogged. If you're using fusible web or a fluffy kind of batting, they may well, after a while start to come through your fabric and stick to the needle. If this happens, just stop what you're doing and wipe off the needle. If it's particularly sticky, a little surgical spirit on a lint free cloth might help. There's not a lot you can really do to prevent this happening although I have found that some types of fusible web and batting are more likely to cause it than others. If you find it an annoyance, just experiment until you get a combination you're happy with.

What Fabrics Can I Use?

Not all fabrics are suitable for free-machine embroidery, so it is important to consider this before you begin. Fabrics have to meet two criteria, what will do the job, and what will look good.

The Importance of Stability

You can use lots of different types of fabrics for free-machine embroidery. I like to use a good mercerized cotton which is stable, easy to sew with and is easily dyed to a colour I like. Unless you're trying to get the sort of effects an unstable fabric will produce when stitched into, you need to make sure your fabric is stable or be prepared to stabilize it by ironing a piece of interfacing onto the back. But if you're just starting out, you don't need the added anxiety of your fabric being difficult to manage, so get yourself a bit of good quality cotton.

However, once you get the hang of embroidery and, if you are into recycling/upcycling and want to cut up and use either your old clothes or those you've sourced from car boot sales and charity shops, then why not? Just make sure the fabric is suitable for what you want to make.

Dyeing Your Own Fabrics

Dyeing your fabric can add a whole new dimension to your embroidery. Some people even dye their own embroidery silks and wind them onto the bobbin. By stitching their fabric upside down the dyed thread will then appear on the right side of the embroidery. Dyeing your own fabrics is not difficult to do, provided you source the right supplies. The most important thing to remember is that cotton, linen and hemp type fabrics are cellulose or vegetable fibres and as such will require a cold water reactive dye such as Procion MX.

Wool and silk are animal or protein, fibres and as such will require an acid dye and a heat source. The dyeing process is outside the scope of this book, but, if you would like to have a go, please see the further reading section.

Stabilizing

Now with free-machine embroidery, whatever fabric you use, if you are not using a hoop, you will need some sort of support for the fabric. If you try and embroider onto fabric without support, it will bunch up, be difficult to manoeuvre and may get pulled under the needle bed, causing a serious jam.

To Hoop...?

If your embroidered piece is to be made into something that does not required a padded backing, such as a pictorial piece or a garment, you may like to use a hoop. This will hold the fabric taught and give you something to hold onto to guide your piece under the needle.

A Standard Embroidery Hoop

A standard two piece wooden embroidery hoop is fine, although if you are working on a large embroidered area which may require moving the hoop to another area, you may prefer to use a quick release hoop as this is less likely to mark your embroidery.

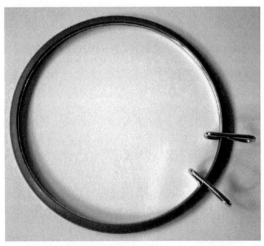

A Quick-Release Hoop

...or not to Hoop?

If your piece is going to be part of something which requires padding or quilting such as a cushion or wall hanging you will need some batting. I use a layer of whichever fabric is going to be the top of the embroidery, a layer of pure cotton batting (the kind you can iron) and a back layer of cheap cotton. The cotton backing is primarily so the cotton batting will not snag on the needle bed. There are those that choose to do without it but I find it useful and, if your embroidered piece is destined to be part of a cushion, I think it is nicer to have a layer of cotton inside rather than just the batting.

Fusible Web

The other, not strictly fabric, item I want to talk about is fusible web, a wonderful product that has truly revolutionised the world of appliqué. There are several types on the market.

Fusible web is essentially a very thin layer of glue with either one or two paper backings. The majority of fusible webs have only one paper backing – the best known being Wonderweb (or Wonder Under in the US) – and these are not pressure sensitive. This means you can't adhere all your bits and pieces of appliqué to your backing fabric before ironing, to see how they look.

I personally prefer Steam-a-Seam which has the glue layer sandwiched in between two layers of paper backing. So when you remove one layer the glue is mildly sticky and can be temporarily attached to fabric. It is also available in two grades, light, which always requires stitching, and standard, which is labelled as 'no-sew'. I always stitch whichever one I use. It is more expensive than the others but I like it for the convenience.

Part 2: Getting Started

Preparing your machine and your fabrics for free-machine embroidery.

Setting Up Your Machine

Now we get to the fun part —the bit where you get to do some sewing. Taking a few moments to set up your sewing machine properly is well worthwhile and will make your embroidery sessions a breeze.

Read the Manual

First of all you need to set up your machine. You'll have already read the previous part telling you all about what you need to do. You'll probably be able to recite your sewing machine manual in your sleep - so let's get the beast up on the table and get started.

Arrange Your Workspace

Arrange you table, chair and machine, ready for work:

1   Make sure the table you're going to be working on is at the right height – if you're working on the dining room table it might be a tad difficult to do any adjustments but adding a few cushions to your chair should help to bring you up to the right level.

2   Make sure you've got adequate lighting and you're wearing the right glasses.

3   Check that the machine is parallel to the front edge of your table and no more than 6" from the edge. On no account have your machine at an angle to the front of the table or so far away that you have to stretch to reach it. This is bad for your back and your sewing.

Have Your Threads at the Ready

Have a few reels of thread ready:

1   An all purpose polyester will be fine for now, as long as it's a good make. There is no point in practising with poor thread as when it starts to snap and shred, you'll be put off before you've even got started.

2   Make sure your bobbin is wound, or have several bobbins in various colours ready if you're not going to want to stop to wind anymore.

Set up Your Machine

Referring to your manual for details, set your machine up for free-machine embroidery:

1   Drop the feed dogs out of use (usually a button on the side, a slider on the back or a switch under the needle bed).

2   Reduce the top tension to somewhere between 0-1.

3   Change the standard sewing foot for machine embroidery or darning foot.

4   Thread your machine top and bottom, bringing the bobbin thread up through the needle plate if necessary.

Angle Your Machine

If you've read the bit about jacking up your sewing machine at the back for a more comfortable sewing position, and you want to try this, now is the time.

1   Remember to use a large format (A4 size) hardback book about ½" deep and insert under the back of your machine to a depth of about 1".

2   Make sure the machine is stable and does not rock back and forth.

Preparing Your Fabric

Fabrics for free-machine embroidery need some preparation and often some support to ensure that you can control your embroidery.

Hooping for Practice

For the purpose of your free-machine embroidery practice session we're going to use a hoop to support the fabric. So you'll need a standard wooden embroidery hoop with quite a low profile, which will easily fit under the presser foot, or a plastic quick release hoop.

To get your fabric ready for stitching:

1   Give your fabric a good steam press and cut it a little larger, all round, than the hoop.

2   Lay the inner ring of the hoop on the table and lay the fabric over it, wrong side up. When you machine embroider, you're going to be stitching on the underside, the recessed part of the fabric and not the topside as in hand embroidery.

3   Now fit the outer ring over the inner ring and fabric and tighten.

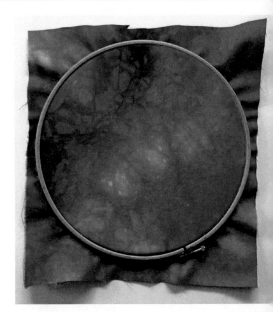

4   Pull the fabric taut evenly all round the outer edge of the hoop but DON'T stretch it. If you stretch your fabric and embroider on it, when you release it from the hoop, it will contract back to its original size, scrunching up your beautiful embroidery in the process.

Let's Sew - Practice Session

You are now ready to sew. You have prepared your workspace, your sewing machine and your fabric and are ready to have a go at free-machine embroidery.

Are You Sitting Comfortably?

Seat yourself in front of the machine so the centre of your body is lined up with the needle, and your forearms, when resting on the needle bed, are at approximately 90 degrees to your body.

Ready to Go!

So you're sat at the machine, hoop in hand, darning foot fitted, feed dogs dropped, all threaded up and ready to go.

1   Slide your hoop under your presser foot, recessed side (and right side of your fabric) facing upwards and position your needle right above the centre of the hooped fabric. You may need to lift your presser foot lever a little higher to allow the hoop to pass underneath.

2   Now hold the top thread in your left hand and turn the hand wheel towards you until the bottom thread is raised to the top. Pull both thread ends clear of the needle bed and hold both securely in your left hand.

3   Lower the presser foot lever. The foot should not rest on the fabric.

4   Now with both threads in your left hand and, at the same time, holding the edges of the hoop in both hands, start stitching over the area where you brought the threads through. Just a few stitches will do to secure the start of your embroidery.

5   Stop and snip off the two long threads at the fabric taking care not to snip the thread you are sewing with.

6   Start stitching again, still holding the hoop in both hands. Try and run the machine at a medium speed and move your hoop round and round in large circles or curves.

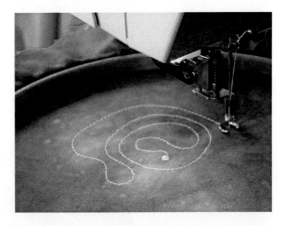

7   Try and keep the machine running at an even
    speed - don't keep stopping and starting –
    although you will at first, we all do! When you
    get a bit more confident try stitching squares
    or even your name.

8   Keep going until you can achieve an even
    machine speed at about half the rate of the
    machine's full speed.

What Are We Trying To Do?

The object of this exercise is to obtain an even
stitch length and this can only be achieved by
running the machine at an even speed and
moving the hoop at an even speed. This can take
a bit of practice and if you can get through this
stage you will go on to love free-machine
embroidery forever. It's not easy; and at first you
will doubt that you will ever manage it. But just
keep on practicing as often as you can, and it will
come.

If you have one of these machines that comes
complete with a stitch regulator foot that senses
how fast you are moving your work and then
adjusts the speed of the machine accordingly to
give you an even stitch length, it is tempting to
think that you don't need to bother with all this
practise palaver. But I would advise you to try it
the old fashioned way, with the standard darning
or embroidery foot and get the hang of that first.

As I've said, time and time again, all this is going
to take time and during that time, you need to be
kind to yourself. It's not a good idea to carry on
without a break, getting more fed up and
frustrated with your apparent lack of progress.
Make sure you take regular breaks, do a few
stretches. Don't beat yourself up, don't say 'I
can't do it' and give it all up. This is a scenario
I've seen so many times, where people expect to
master free-free-machine embroidery in just one
session. This is a shame as with a bit of staying
power those same people could easily go on to
enjoy a lifelong hobby.

If it's not going well, stop. Get a fresh piece of
fabric and try again. If you don't like using a
hoop, iron your fabric over a bit of cotton batting
and a bit of cotton backing, secure with a few
quilter's safety pins, and try embroidering this
way. The only risk here is without the barrier of
the hoop, you may be tempted to move your
hands closer to the needle. Constantly remind
yourself to only hold your fabric by the edges,
particularly at this stage where you are
concentrating hard on getting your machine
speed, and the speed you move your fabric, in
harmony.

Part 3: Appliqué

Using free-machine embroidery and appliqué to embellish your sewing.

Appliqué – Ideas and Inspirations

The first thing you have to think about when considering using free-machine embroidery for appliqué, which is my favourite technique of all, is what you want to make. The possibilities are endless, but I would say, try and narrow it down to a few simple starter projects.

Cushions

Firstly, consider a cushion. Cushions are great canvases for any sort of design and are useful as well as decorative.

I have to confess to making almost all cushions. I use words, images, logos and even found objects such as newsprint or packaging.

Wall Hangings

You might even consider making a small wall hanging. Wall hangings can be a good starting point for your first efforts in free-machine embroidery as you can hang them in your craft room or corner and they will remind you of your tentative beginnings and how far you have come.

Notebook Covers

If you prefer something smaller for your first project you could consider a notebook. When I'm not machine-embroidering, I like to write so I've always got a notebook on the go. A nice machine embroidered cover can make the cheapest of notebooks into something precious and personal

Clothing

Perhaps you'd prefer to decorate an existing article. If you have a baby, young child or grandchild, you may like to add a motif or design to an item of their clothing, or even a bib or comforter. Aprons can also be great canvases for appliqué designs. You could add a few vegetables or food items to make a personal gift for a friend or relative who loves to cook.

Bags

Bags make another great foil for appliqué designs and are great for showing off your newly acquired skills to the world. I love making bags of all styles.

Choosing a Design

Once you've decided what it is you want to make, you need to decide on a design, a shape or an image and, I would say at this point, make it very simple. It will do wonders for your confidence to do something simple really well, rather than to attempt something difficult and be disappointed when it is not quite perfect.

The classic beach hut is a great iconic image and shape and I've given you a project at the end of this chapter, using a beach hut image – you'll love it.

Appliqué – Techniques and Skills

A little practice before the big event will help you to develop the required skills and boost your confidence. Work through the practice piece below to create your first appliquéd design.

Where Can I Find Images?

If you're having trouble finding a shape or image and you've told yourself you're no good at drawing, why not look for something suitable on the internet? There are plenty of sites offering royalty-free images.

There is also a selection of appliqué images on my website at www.time4me-workshops.co.uk.

You may have some photos of your own that you could simplify. You could use a simple image from a greetings card. If your image is very small, I would suggest enlarging it on a photocopier until it is at least 4" x 6".

Practice Piece

When you have selected an image for your practice piece:

1 Get yourself a piece of fusible web, large enough to cover the image completely. At this stage I would just use the outline of the complete image, rather than dividing it up into different coloured areas.

2 Trace the image onto the fusible web. If you are using fusible web with one paper backing, lay it onto the image glue side down and trace onto the paper side using a standard HB pencil.

3 Now prepare your backing fabric by giving it a good press. The size of the backing piece will depend on what you've decided to make. If you're making a cushion, make it small to start with, about 10" square.

4 Cut a piece of pure cotton batting about ½" larger than the backing fabric all the way round.

Note:
The pure cotton batting, if you can get it, is much better for appliqué than the expanded polyester stuff. It lies flatter and can be ironed as many times as you like. It is also preferable for babies and children and, as cotton is a poor conductor of heat, it is warm in winter and cool in summer.

5 Then get a bit of cheap cotton backing, doesn't really matter about the colour as it's not going to be seen.

6 Layer them together, background fabric on the top, batting in the middle and backing on the bottom and give them a good press. You will find that the background and backing fabric will stick lightly to the batting making the whole sandwich quite stable.

7 Now press your appliqué fabric and, if it has a right and wrong side, place your fusible web with the traced image on, glue side down onto the wrong side of the fabric. If you are using fusible web with two paper backings you will need to remove one backing before you press the web onto the fabric. Ensure the glue layer remains with the paper backing onto which you traced the image.

Note:
To avoid getting glue on your iron, place the appliqué fabric with the fusible web on top onto the ironing board and cover the shape with a piece of thin cotton cloth.

8   Refer to the instructions for your particular brand of fusible web and press, rather than iron it onto the fabric.

9   Carefully cut out your appliqué shape and remove the remaining paper backing.

10 Remove the remaining paper backing.

11 Place the background fabric, with the appliqué shape in the position you want it, onto the ironing board and press, with the cotton pressing cloth in place (if using), until the shape is firmly adhered.

12 Lay the whole piece on to your table (not onto a cutting mat as the pins will get stuck in the mat) and position some quilter's safety pins around your image, about 2" apart.

13 Stitch around your image, using an embroidery thread of your choice, two or three times. Avoid trying to place each layer of stitching exactly on top of the one below, as if you achieve this most of the time, the places where you do wander off may look a little odd. Better to try and keep them close together and on your appliqué shape rather than wandering off the edge.

31

Note:
Don't get too hung up on being too neat. The whole point of raw edge appliqué is that is meant to look naive and folky. Don't aim for perfection as handmade isn't about perfection. Handmade is the little quirks of a piece that make it so endearing to the buying public, the same public who prefer to buy one-off unique pieces that aren't churned out by some factory in the far east.

Once you have completed your outline, you may want to add some other embroidered details. These can be drawn on with tailor's chalk or an air-dissolving pen and then stitched.

If you are stitching a number of details in the same colour thread, there is no need to cut the thread between each detail. When you are finished stitching one area just do a few reverse stitches to secure, lift your presser foot, move to the next area, do a few securing stitches and stitch on. The 'jump' threads can be trimmed when you have finished all your stitching.

Now let's move on to your first free-machine embroidery project!

Project - Beach Hut Notebook Cover

Notebooks are available in a wide range of designs but there is nothing more personal than making your own removable notebook cover.

You Will Need

- **1 piece of blue cotton fabric measuring at least 17" (43cm) x 6½" (16 5cm).**
- **1 piece of yellow cotton fabric measuring at least 17" (43cm) x 5½" (14cm).**
- **1 piece pure cotton wadding measuring at least 18" (46cm) x 12" (30cm).**
- **1 piece lightweight cotton backing measuring at least 18" (46cm) x 12" (30cm).**
- **Fabric scraps in red and green for beach hut appliqué.**
- **Fusible web for beach hut appliqué.**
- **Machine embroidery and polyester thread in beach hut colours.**

- **A5 hardback notebook with spine (not spiral bound).**

Hand-Dyed Fabrics
A range of hand-dyed cotton fabrics are available from www.time4me-workshops.co.uk/shop.

Machine Setup

All seam allowances are ¼" (1cm) unless stated otherwise.

A 2.5mm stitch length is used throughout except for the addition of appliqué images.

A standard zig-zag foot is used throughout unless stated otherwise.

To Make Your Cover

Cut Your Pattern Pieces

1   From the blue cotton fabric, cut a rectangle 17" (43cm) x 6½" (16 5cm).

2   From the yellow cotton fabric, cut a rectangle 17" (43cm) x 5½" (14cm).

Make Your Background Fabric

3   Place the two rectangles wrong sides together, lining up one of the long edges. Pin

and stitch the long edge. Press the seam open.

4   Cut the cotton batting so it is ½" larger all round than the background fabric.

5   Cut the cotton backing so it is ½" larger all round than the background fabric.

6   Lay the backing fabric on a flat surface, place the batting on top, right side up (the bumpy side is usually the right side) and then the background piece on top, right side up.

Cutting Out Your Appliqué Shapes

7   Take the fusible web and, on the paper side, draw a rectangle 5" x 3".

8   Now mark halfway along the top 3" line and 1½" from the top of both 5" lines as shown in the diagram. This is the main beach hut shape.

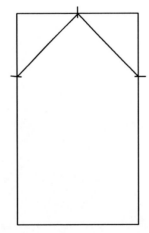

9   For the door, draw a rectangle 2" x 1" and for the roof edges draw 2 x rectangles ½" x 3".

10 Roughly cut out the rectangles and the beach hut front.

11 Press the fabric scraps.

12 In accordance with the instructions for the brand of fusible web you are using, fuse the beach hut rectangle to the back of the red fabric and the roof and door rectangles to the back of the green.

13 Carefully cut out each rectangle and set aside.

Attach Your Image

14 Measure the depth of the spine of the notebook you are intending to cover. Divide this figure in two and make a note of the result.

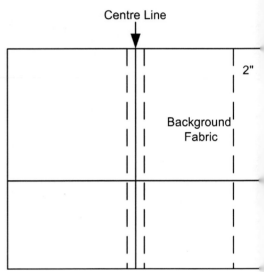

15 Now take the layered background fabric and mark the centre line as shown in the diagram.

16 Mark a line either side of the centre line, of the measurement taken earlier (half the depth of the spine).

17 Now mark a line 2" in from the right hand edge of the background fabric as shown in the diagram.

18 The area between the two right hand dotted lines will be your front cover. It may help to fold the book cover around the notebook and tuck in the 2" flap as shown below'

19 Place your beach hut main shape centrally within the front cover area and place the roof edges and door on top. Fuse in place.

Stitch Your Appliqué in Place

20 Set your machine up for free-machine embroidery and thread up with the red embroidery thread on top and the red polyester on the bobbin.

21 Starting just under the roof edge, stitch down one side of the main beach hut shape, along the bottom edge, avoiding the door, and up the other side stopping at the roof and working a few securing stitches. Repeat so you have two rows of stitching, but place the second row next to rather than on top of the first.

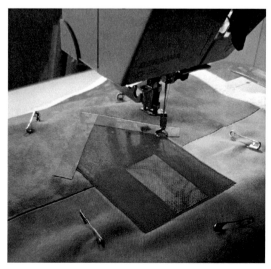

22 Using tailor's chalk, draw vertical lines, ½" apart, down the main beach hut shape.

23 Stitch over these lines, twice, starting at the bottom of the first one and stitching to the top, following the roof edge to the next line and stitching to the bottom, then along the bottom to the next line etc. This means you won't have to break your thread or form any jump loops between lines.

24 Press the panel thoroughly but don't concentrate too much heat on the embroidery stitching as it may melt.

25 Trim the panel to 17" x 10½".

26 Pin the layers together all the way round the panel, placing the pins at 90 degrees to the edges.

27 Set your machine for a full width (this will depend on the make of your machine) and 2mm length zig-zag stitch. Stitch all round the panel, doing a few reverse stitches at the end to secure.

28 Press again to flatten the zig-zagged edges.

Assembling the Cover

29 Lay the stitched panel face up on a flat surface. Turn in a 2" flap at each side of the panel. Press lightly.

30 Now measure ¾" from the top and bottom of the 2" flaps, mark with tailor's chalk and place a pin at 90 degrees to the line, pinning through all the layers.

31 At this stage it is a good idea to check that your book will fit into the cover, while it is still inside out, and will close once in. If it is a little tight and won't close completely, reduce the size of the 2" flaps a little until it does.

32 Now using a 2.5mm straight stitch, stitch across the ¾" lines at the top and bottom of each flap. Do a few reverse stitches at the beginning and end of each line of stitching to secure.

33 Turn your book cover right side out, pushing out the corners so they look square.

34 Press thoroughly, ensuring that the turned-in edges top and bottom are the same depth across the width of the cover.

35 If you wish, you can add a button or other decoration to the beach hut door.

36 Insert your book into the cover and treasure!

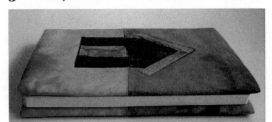

Part 4: Writing with a Needle

Using free-machine embroidery to add words to your sewing.

Writing with a Needle - Ideas and Inspirations

There are ideas for decorative writing everywhere. You just need to know where to look.

Where to Find Inspiration

The Shopping Mall

When we shop, most of us don't pay much attention to the advertising blurb that is pushed in front of our faces as we are normally more concerned with what we are going to buy. But text, lettering, words, it's all around us. Without realising it we are attracted by some types of text and put off by others. Some designs of text (or fonts) are designed to appeal to women, some to men and lots to children. Even children who are too young to read are attracted to the clever manipulation of shapes and colours that make up simple words. Words are so evocative. They can make us think of Christmas, summer holidays, food, toys and games.

So the next time you're out shopping, take some time to look at the words around you, the fonts they are written in and the effect they have on you. Are they something you could use in your work? Take a photo of those you like best and arrange them into a digital album to refer to when you're in need of a new idea.

Historical Books

Everyone has a favourite period in history. Even if they don't know much about it and are not too hot on the dates and details, they have seen something on TV or in a newspaper or book that has chimed with them and made them think 'I could have lived then'.

Now my favourite historical period is the medieval age. I know that, fond as I am of my 21st Century comforts, I would have struggled to live then. But when I look at the illuminated manuscripts with their painstakingly-formed, curlicue-adorned letters and colourful scenes of chivalric life, I want to recreate them in stitch.

I have always told myself that one day, having seen the original (in Bayeux, France) and the Victorian copy (in Reading Museum in the UK), I would create my own local version of the Bayeux Tapestry – that great embroidered work telling the story of the Norman Conquest. I have heard - and seen the work of a tenacious group in Scotland who have created a hand–embroidered history of a local battle… but I have yet to get started.

So if you are interested in a particular period in history, you don't have to scour specialist libraries or apply for permission to view the original documents. There is a wealth of reprinted historical material available in many lending libraries. I have just returned a large format version of 'The Anglo-Saxon Chronicles' to my local library.

But whatever period you choose and however you choose to study it, look at the lettering. Any form of text is not difficult to recreate in text. You could even use the original letters as a starting point and go on to create your own fantastic alphabet.

Calligraphy Books

Calligraphy was once the method by which medieval monks and scribes created the great texts that we so treasure today. But now it has become a popular hobby amongst card and sig makers and there is a huge range of books available showing the different types of lettering and the way each letter is formed. As you can imagine, these are very useful for embroiderers wanting to use decorative lettering in their work.

The Internet

Of course, examples of all the sources I have mentioned are widely available on the internet along with examples of unusual and themed fonts. You don't even have to leave the comfort of your own home to access more inspiration than you will ever need in a hundred lifetimes. But I like going out to do my research. There is something special about seeing things in the context for which they were intended and that context may help you to plan the perfect project to display your embroidered letters.

Writing with a Needle – Skills and Techniques

Writing with a sewing machine may seem a bit ambitious but, with a little planning and practice, anyone can master this technique.

Get it into Your Head

Some time ago, I read that the best way to ensure accurate free-machine embroidery is to first of all get the image, of whatever you're going to embroider, into your brain. Doing this will ensure that your brain is subconsciously going to envisage that shape when you start to embroider. Now however odd this sounds, it does work. I can testify to that – and not just with letters either.

Practice Piece

Writing with a needle can be very effective but this is something else that takes a bit of practice. First of all you need to decide what it is that you want to write. Once you have:

1   Write it out, several times, on a piece of paper and use a copperplate type font (old-fashioned joined-up writing). It's easier to follow than block letters with its curves and you won't need to be jumping between letters.

2   Trace over the letters several times with your finger, from start to finish, trying not to think too hard about what you're doing.

3   If, after all this tracing it out with a finger, you still don't think you're going to be able to stitch your letters accurately, you can try drawing out the letters with an air dissolving pen. You can use water soluble if that's all you have but I would rather avoid having to rinse out the writing afterwards.

Note:
The only drawback with an air-soluble pen is that they can start to fade within an hour or two. So if you you're going to make it to the end of your stitching before the pen lines have disappeared, don't write your words out until just before you're about to start stitching. And make sure you iron your fabric before you draw with the air soluble pen otherwise the ironing tends to set the pen marks and you will end up having to wash them out.

Once you've tried this with copperplate, you may decide you want to try it in block letters. So follow the same process again. Write it out; follow it with your finger and stitch.

When you're stitching out individual letters it really isn't worth stopping to cut the thread between each letter. So when you're doing block letters, go over each one twice then do a few stitches back and forth at the end of the letter jump to the next letter, few stitches back and forth to secure and off you go leaving the 'jump loops' until you have reached the end of your stitching.

Don't worry if when stitching you don't follow the lines exactly. This is a handmade piece, made with love and a few little wobbles are what makes it personal - your own work.

I've designed a little laundry bag here which will not only give you some practice in writing with a needle but will also bolster your appliqué skills!.

Project - Washday Laundry Bag

Make this fun laundry bag in any colour or size you want. If you want to make one for everyone in the family, why not personalise it with their names?

You Will Need

- **½m strong cotton fabric**
- **Fabric scraps for washing appliqué**
- **Fusible web for washing appliqué**
- **Machine embroidery and polyester thread in black**
- **2m cotton cord**
- **Embroidery hoop**

Hand-Dyed Fabrics
A range of hand-dyed cotton fabrics are available from www.time4me-workshops.co.uk/shop.

Machine Setup

All seam allowances are ½" (1.25cm) unless stated otherwise.

A 2.5mm stitch length is used throughout except for the addition of appliqué images.

A standard zig-zag foot is used throughout unless otherwise stated.

To Make Your Laundry Bag

Cut Your Pattern Pieces

1 From the cotton fabric, cut 2 x rectangles 19" (48cm) x 16" (41cm).

2 From the remaining cotton fabric, cut 2 x strips 2" x 20".

Appliqué Your Front Panel

3 Choose one of the rectangles to be the front panel and lay it on a flat surface with one of the shortest edges at the bottom.

4 Measure 8" from the bottom edge of each long (19") side and mark these points.

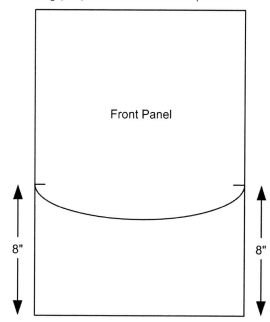

5 Using a dressmaker's curve or curved ruler and some tailor's chalk, draw a curved line between these points. This will be the position of the washing line.

6 On the paper side of your fusible web, draw an assortment of clothing or soft toys you might find on your washing line. These do not have to be artistically correct – have fun!

7 Roughly cut out each shape.

> **Note:**
> If the recipient has a favourite toy, pyjamas or t-shirt, you could make one of the pieces a similar shape and colour.

8 Choose the colours of your washing items from your fabric scraps and iron each piece.

9 Referring to the instructions for the brand of fusible web you are using, fuse each clothing shape onto the wrong side of your chosen fabrics and carefully cut out.

10 Arrange your washing with the top edges just slightly below the curved line until you are happy with it.

11 Fuse in place.

12 Refer to your machine instruction manual and set your machine up for free-machine embroidery, fit an embroidery or darning foot and thread the top with black embroidery thread and the bobbin with black polyester thread.

13 Hoop your fabric, so a number of complete washing items are encircled (this will depend on the size of your hoop). Ensure your appliqué is on the recessed side of the hoop.

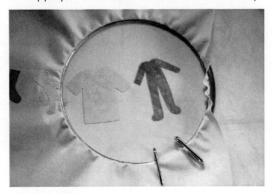

14 Embroider around each article of clothing, adding details as required.

15 Add pegs to each clothing item or toy.

16 Refer to your instruction manual and set your sewing machine for normal stitching. Fit a standard straight stitch/zig-zag foot to your machine and using a 3mm length straight stitch, stitch several times over the line marked earlier for the position of the washing line.

Add Your Writing

17 Using a ruler and tailor's chalk, draw a straight line connecting the two ends of the washing line.

18 Mark the central point of the line and from this point, draw a box 7" x 3", so the bottom 7" edge of the box rests on the line. Your embroidered word, whatever you have chosen, should fit inside this box, but if you are using a longer name or several words you may need to increase the size of the box accordingly (and the size of your hoop).

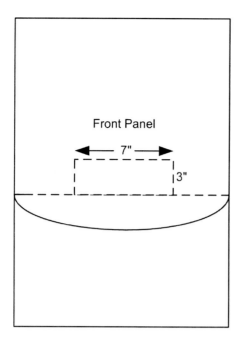

Front Panel

← 7" →

3"

19 Now, on a sheet of paper, draw out the 7" x 3" box and write the word you are intending to embroider inside in a neat copperplate. Try to ensure there is an equal amount of space above and below the word.

20 Once you are happy with your word, trace over it a number of times with your finger as described in the previous section.

21 Place your front panel in the hoop, centralising the box as accurately as possible.

22 Set your machine for free-machine embroidery as before, and embroider your word. Don't worry if you go off a little here and there, this will only add a little homemade charm.

Assemble Your Laundry Bag

23 Place the bag front and back panels right sides together and pin round the two sides and the bottom.

24 Set your sewing machine for a 2.5mm straight stitch and stitch round the three sides.

25 Diagonally clip the two bottom corners.

26 Press open the side seams.

27 Turn over ¼" all round the top of the bag and press.

28 Turn over another ¾" and press again.

29 Place some pins at 90 degrees around the top of the bag and stitch close to the lower fold. Turn the bag right way out, pushing out the corners.

30 Now stitch together the two 2" strips along one of their short ends and press the seam open. Trim the length of the strip to 32". This strip will be your cord casing.

31 Turn in ½" on each short edge of the strip and press.

32 Turn in ¼" on each long edge of the strip and press.

33 Using tailor's chalk, mark a line 2" below the top edge, all the way round the bag.

34 Starting at the right hand side seam (with the front panel facing you) pin the pressed strip, with the raw edges facing the bag, all round the bag, finishing back at the side seam. Try and place the seam, in the pressed strip, at the rear of the bag.

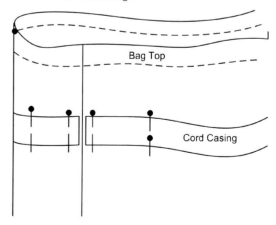

Bag Top

Cord Casing

35 Stitch all round both long edges of the cord casing about 1/8" from the edge, working a

few reverse stitches at the beginning and end of each seam to secure.

36 Apply a piece of sticky tape to each end of your cotton cord to prevent fraying while threading it through the casing.

37 Using a large safety pin, fastened to one end of the cord, thread it through the casing and knot the ends together securely. Remove the tape as fraying is limited by the position of the knot.

38 The bag looks better filled, so get your family to fill it with their laundry.

Part 5: Free-Motion Quilting

Using free-machine embroidery to quilt your sewing.

Free-Motion Quilting – Ideas and Inspirations

There are ideas for quilting designs everywhere but which one is suitable for your quilt?

What Do You Want to Make?

Quilting with free-machine embroidery is generally called free-motion quilting. The stitching technique is much the same but it is normally carried out on a larger finished or almost finished article. These articles are usually quilts of some design but they could also be throws, cushions or wall-hangings.

How you are going to free-motion quilt your project depends, of course, on what it is. If it is a large, plain piece of fabric, or a wholecloth quilt, then you can pretty much do what you want. If you are making and quilting a patchwork quilt it is important not to overwhelm the patchwork with too much stitching.

Some quilts are striking enough already and only require a simple meandering design to add an extra textural element.

If you have a quilt with alternating plain and patterned panels you may like to make a feature of the plain panels by adding some stitching that fits in with the theme of the patterned fabric.

Finding Inspiration

Inspiration is everywhere for quilting images. You could consider using elements of the following natural forms:

- Birds
- Trees
- Flowers
- Leaves
- Vines
- Tendrils

Or you could look at man-made structures such as buildings, paving designs and bridges for examples of:

- Tiles
- Spirals
- Circles
- Squares

If you want to make a quilt, throw or even some Christmas stockings for the festive season, you could use some sparkly or self-patterned fabric and quilt some stars or Christmas trees all over for a subtle design.

If you are keen to take your inspiration from things that you see when you're out and about, you could carry a small sketchbook. Or if sketching is not your thing (and I'm with you on this one) maybe carry a small camera to record your findings.

There are a number of good books on the subject of designing for free-motion embroidery on quilts and I have listed a few at the back of this book. There is also, of course, the internet, where a bit of basic searching will bring you many designs that you can draw inspiration from.

Free-Motion Quilting – Skills and Techniques

You will be securing three layers together, as in a quilt or throw, using free-machine embroidery. Again, a little forethought and preparation can yield fantastic results.

What's the Difference?

Using free-motion quilting on a large quilt or throw needs more care and securing with pins as over a larger area the fabric is more likely to move. Generally, you will be securing three larger layers together as in a quilt or throw. The first thing you need to do is choose a design that will complement your quilt. There are lots of books about this subject and it is beyond the scope of this book to consider every possible method and pattern for quilting your quilt. This is just intended to be a basic introduction to the subject. If you enjoy it, I suggest you check out some of the books I've listed in the further reading section at the end of this book.

Sketch out Your Design

Once you've decided on a design for your quilt – it might just be a simple corner to corner it might just be stitching in the ditch but if you've decided on a free-Motion design - you need to draw it out first to ensure it is going to fit comfortably into the space that you've intended it for. A good way of doing this is to use one of those child's magnetic drawing tablets like Etch-a-Sketch or Magnadoodle. This way you don't need any paper, just keep drawing it out and wiping it off until you are happy with the result. The other alternative, if you have the technology, is to use an iPad drawing app, of which there are many.

Keep It Simple

I would advise that if you are new to this way of quilting, choose something simple – the simpler the better. Something simple done well is going to look much better than something complicated done not so well. But I wouldn't worry too much about small mistakes. Once you been close to your quilt, embroidering it all day you are going to see every little mistake but if you throw it over the back of the sofa before you go to bed, you'll be amazed how few of them you notice when you come down in the morning.

Stencils and Chalk Markers

If you're not comfortable drawing things freehand, you can use stencils and a chalk marker to temporarily mark your design and they will brush off after stitching. The only drawback with these is that they sometimes get brushed off while you are stitching and you might have to redraw them half way through. But generally, I have heard good reports about them so it is worth a try. You can of course use a water or air soluble pen as discussed later.

Practice Pieces

Now I've given you a few simple designs to practice with. The basics ones are squares, circles and even simple flowers, tiles or wavy lines. But whatever you do decide to do on your fist piece, keep it simple. It will boost your confidence.

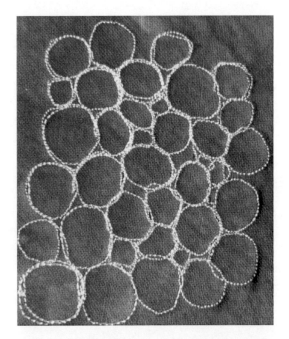

Circles give a pebble-like effect.

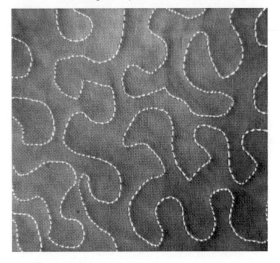

Vermicelli looks good over a large area.

Use the Right Threads

As regards threads, I like to see the quilted effect, so I tend to use a harmonising thread colour which will accentuate the quilted areas rather than the stitching. And it will also hide any mistakes in the stitching! If it's a multi-coloured quilt that you've patched, or a multicoloured fabric, use a neutral thread as that's not going to jump out you and the quilted areas will still be accentuated. On the back I would either use a neutral colour or something that will match your backing fabric. The only problem with having different colours on the top and bottom of your

work is that if your tension is not spot on you risk being able to see the bottom thread on the top of the work. But you can adjust your tension accordingly until this no longer happens. So experiment a bit.

As regards thread composition, a polyester thread which, with its round profile does not reflect much light, will be fairly invisible, if it is a neutral colour and will appear to sink into the work. If you really want to see the stitching use machine embroidery thread which will reflect more light and add an extra dimension to your quilt. If you want to use cotton make sure it's a good quality 100% cotton quilting thread. Cheap cotton threads will produce a lot of lint and will clog up your machine and needle and you won't get the good finish you'd hoped for.

There are many books specialising in free-motion quilting. I've hopefully whetted your appetite enough to get you moving onto more complex projects. Whatever you do – enjoy!

.

Project – Log Cabin Sampler

Get in some serious free-motion embroidery practice with this little sampler.

You Will Need

- **A selection of mixed non-stretch fabrics – cottons, nets, silks etc**
- **Piece of cotton batting 21" (54cm) x 21" (54cm)**
- **Piece of cotton backing 21" (54cm) x 21" (54cm)**
- **Piece of toning cotton for binding, at least 22" (58cm) x 12" (30cm)**
- **Machine embroidery and polyester threads**

> **Hand-Dyed Fabrics**
> A range of hand-dyed cotton fabrics are available from www.time4me-workshops.co.uk/shop.

Machine Setup

All seam allowances are ¼" unless stated otherwise.

A 2.5mm stitch length is used throughout except for the addition of appliqué images.

A standard zig-zag foot is used throughout unless otherwise stated.

To Make Your Log Cabin Sampler

Cut Your Log Cabin Strips

1 This project does not require accurate cutting or measuring and its charm lies in its slightly lop-sided and off-centre look.

2 From your selection of fabrics cut 4 squares or rectangles for the centre of each log cabin panel.

3 Cut several strips of varying widths and lengths from the remaining fabric. You can always cut more as you need them.

4 Cut 4 x strips 3" x 22" from the binding fabric.

Make Your Log Cabin Panels

5 Choose one of the squares or rectangles cut in the first step and lay it, right side up on a flat surface.

6 Take one of the strips and lay it face down on the square with one of the short edges flush with the edge of the square.

7 Trim the strip to the same length of the square.

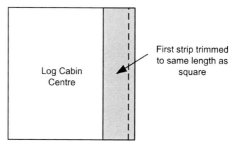

Log Cabin Centre

First strip trimmed to same length as square

8 Stitch as shown in diagram leaving a ¼" seam allowance.

9 Open out strip and press, ensuring the seam allowance is pressed towards the strip.

10 Take a second strip and apply as shown below.

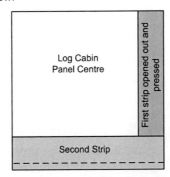

11 Continue adding strips in this manner, cutting more as required and adding a mixture of fabrics and colours, always moving in a clockwise direction until your panel measures approximately 12" square. The number of strips required will depend on how wide you have cut them

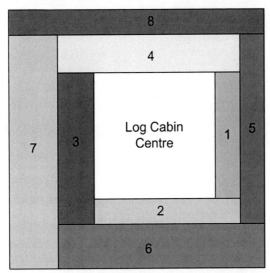

12 Make 3 further panels in the same manner but mixing up the fabrics a bit so all panels look a little different.

13 When all your panels are complete, press them thoroughly and then trim each one to an 11" square.

14 Lay the squares out until you are pleased with the arrangement.

15 Lay one of the squares from the top row face down on top of the other square in the top row. Pin, stitch and press the seam open.

16 Repeat with the second row.

17 Matching up the centre seam, lay one row face down on the other. Pin, stitch and press this seam open.

18 Press your panel thoroughly and trim to a 20" square.

Add Some Free-Motion Embroidery

19 Press the square of cotton backing and lay it face down on a flat surface. Lay the cotton batting on top. Lay your panel on top of this, face up. Press the whole sandwich to enable the layers to cling together.

20 Using, curved dressmakers pins, pin all three layers together, placing pins about 6" apart.

21 Referring to your instruction manual, set your machine up for free machine embroidery and thread as required ensuring you use a toning polyester thread in the bobbin.

22 Add embroidery to each square and strip in the panel. Here are some examples of stitches you could use:

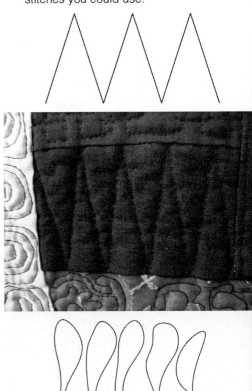

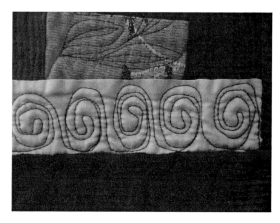

23 You can also use squares, swirls, spirals circles and waves (as shown in the Ideas and Techniques section of this chapter).Experiment with stitches of your own but try and keep each type of stitching on a single strip. Try not to be too prescriptive about making sure your stitching is perfect. The whole aim of this piece is to have fun and make something that is uniquely yours!

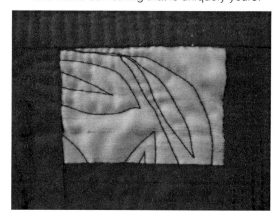

Add Your Binding

24 Take your four binding strips, fold them in half lengthways, and press.

25 Lay one of the binding strips onto one of the panel edges, raw edges together. Pin, placing the pins at 90 degrees to the panel edge.

26 Repeat on the opposite panel edge.

27 Trim the ends of the binding strips flush with the edges of the panel.

28 Stitch through all the layers, ¼" from the raw edges.

29 Flip the binding over to the back of the quilt and press.

30 Now fold the binding over until the folded edge meets the line of stitching. Press and pin in place, placing the pins in line with the binding.

31 Apply the remaining binding strips to the two remaining edges, leaving 1" overhang at each end. Stitch in place.

32 Turn the 1" overhang, at each end, inwards and then fold binding as before, to form a perfect corner. Pin and stitch in place using small, neat slip stitches.

Part 6: Drawing Pictures

Using free-machine embroidery to create artistic textile pictures.

Drawing Pictures - Ideas and Inspiration

Free-machine embroidery can be used to create wonderful freehand sketches or line drawings. The possibilities are endless and this technique enables you to bring your own distinctive artistic flair to your sewing.

Choosing a Design

Creating pictures with free-machine embroidery is something I'm particularly fond of.

A street scene of Victorian houses with a few areas picked out in appliqué and the outlines embroidered in a black thread, can be very endearing. The stitching needn't be over-complicated to achieve the desired effect and simpler designs can actually be even more effective than those which have been laboured over for days.

Birds, flowers and trees are also very suitable for this type of free-embroidery as their simple outlines are immediately recognisable and the addition of some colour and detail can easily make particular species identifiable.

Once you get used to the technique, and if you have a transport-loving family, you could try embroidering trains, cars, motorbikes and bicycles.

Inspiration

The best sort of inspiration for this type of embroidery is that which you are attempting to recreate in stitch – the simple sketch. There are many books of sketches of houses with wobbly lines and scant detail and these are ideal.

You don't need to, and indeed should not attempt to copy them line for line. But spending time looking over drawings of images, similar to the ones you would like to stitch, will give you a feel for the process.

Drawing Pictures - Skills and Techniques

Wobbly lines and scant detail are the order of the day when it comes to creating pictures.

Why Wobbly Lines?

Creating single line pictures using machine embroidery is not an architectural exercise but really a kind of naïve art. The lines you stitch and the appliqué you add are a suggestion of the scene you have chosen for your inspiration. Real trees are not composed of a few squiggles and a splodge of green paint just as houses(at least the brick built ones) have more than a few bricks in each wall.

But by depicting these features in the way I have suggested, we can be sure that the viewer knows what is intended.

So don't worry if your stitching is a little off or your line has wobbled or wandered further than you intended. It's all part of the charm.

Adding Appliqué

The amount of appliqué you add to a picture is entirely up to you. Some scenes which have a lot of detail, such as churches or cathedrals, can benefit from just the odd touch of colour, leaving their serene beauty to shine through in just the stitching alone.

Some scenes, such as naive houses, buses or trains can benefit from having large, simple blocks of colour added. This can add significantly to the quirkyness of the project and can place the scene in the era which it was intended.

The cushion below uses bright modern colours giving the sense of up-market town houses in a modern city.

While the following cushion uses muted chalky shades which give a sense of an older Victorian or Georgian street.

But appliqué need not be used just to add colour, it can also be valuable for adding shading to the side of a building. This can help in preventing a scene from looking too flat. I have used this technique in the Tearoom Cushion project which follows.

Project – Tea Room Cushion

Picture your perfect tea shop. The image shown here is just an example of the type of embroidery that would look good on a cushion. You can use any image you think is suitable or copy the one I have used. The embroidered image does not have to be perfect, in fact the effect is enhanced by a few squiggly lines.

You Will Need

- **Piece of strong cotton fabric at least 12" (30cm) x 16" (41cm) for front panel**
- **½m of strong cotton fabric for rear panel and piping**
- **Piece of cotton batting at least 12" (30cm) x 16" (41cm)**
- **Piece of thin cotton backing at least 12" (30cm) x 16" (41cm)**
- **Fabric scraps for house appliqué**
- **Fusible web for house appliqué**
- **Machine embroidery and polyester thread in washing hut colours**
- **1½ m piping cord**
- **12" nylon zip in a toning colour**

Hand-Dyed Fabrics
A range of hand-dyed cotton fabrics are available from www.time4me-workshops.co.uk/shop.

Machine Setup

All seam allowances are ½" (1.25cm) unless stated otherwise.

A 2.5mm stitch length is used throughout except for the addition of appliqué images.

A standard zig-zag foot is used throughout unless otherwise stated.

To Make Your Cushion

Cut Your Pattern Pieces

1   From the front panel cotton fabric, cut 1 x rectangle 12" x 16".

2   From the rear panel cotton fabric, cut 2 x rectangles 6½" x 16".

3   From the cotton batting, cut 1 x rectangle 12½" x 16½".

4   From the cotton backing, cut 1 x rectangle 12½" x 16½".

Appliqué Your Front Panel

5   Choose a suitable image for your embroidery. The simpler the sketch, the easier you will find it to copy onto your fabric

6   Press your front panel and thin cotton backing. Lay the backing on a flat surface then lay the batting on top followed by the front panel. Press the sandwich thoroughly to help them to adhere together.

Note:
It is important to press the layers together before you draw your image on. I have found that if you use an air-soluble pen, ironing over it will set the ink and make it more difficult to remove.

7   If your chosen image is smaller than your cushion panel, you may need to enlarge it o a photocopier until it is about 2" smaller all

round than the panel. If you want to use the image I've used, enlarge the photo about 500%.

8 Using an air soluble pen, lightly sketch the main outline of your chosen image. If you would like to add some coloured fabric appliqué to the image, as I have done, do this now.

Note:
If the area you want to appliqué is not symmetrical, as in the case of my image, you will need to ensure that you trace a mirror image onto your fusible web. You can do this by tracing the area onto tracing paper, turning the tracing paper over then going over the image again to copy it onto your fusible web.

9 When you have cut out and fused your image onto the area you want to appliqué, work two lines of black embroidery round the edges. Try and introduce a little wobble into your stitching!

Embroider Your Remaining Image

10 Now embroider two lines around all the other outlines of your image.

11 Draw in roof details, chimneys and a few blocks of bricks to suggest masonry. Embroider.

12 Add windows, curtains and doors and any shrubbery.

13 Lastly, draw any lettering and embroider. Don't worry if you go off a little – it will add a little handmade charm.

14 Once your embroidered image is complete, set it aside for the remainder of the air-soluble pen to dissolve.

15 Trim all the layers to a 12" x 16" rectangle.

Note:
If you must press your front panel, do so as lightly as possible. If you completely flatten the image, the relief effect will be lost.

Insert Your Zip

16 Place the two cushion back panels right sides together.

17 Lay your zip centrally down one long edge of the panels

18 Using tailor's chalk, mark, on the cushion fabric, where the zip teeth begin and end.

19 Reset your sewing machine to a 2.5mm straight stitch with a standard zig-zag foot and the feed dogs raised.

20 Using a ½" seam allowance, stitch from the edge of the fabric to this mark.

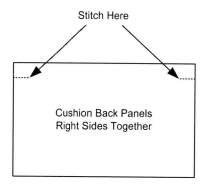

Stitch Here

Cushion Back Panels
Right Sides Together

21 Press entire seam allowance open from one seam to the other.

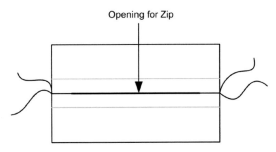

Opening for Zip

22 Turn over the joined panels and lay them on a flat surface.

23 Place the zip in the opening between the seams and pin the left-hand folded edge of the fabric close to the teeth of the zip.

24 Lap the right-hand edge slightly over the left-hand edge and pin in place, placing the pins against the teeth.

25 Tack all round the zip and remove the pins.

26 Fit a zipper foot onto your sewing machine and move the needle to the right side of the foot.

Note:
On some types of sewing machine, you may need to move the position of the foot rather than the needle.

27 Open the zip to a distance of 2". Beginning at the edge of the fabric nearest the top of the zip, stitch the left-hand side of the zip, ensuring you catch in the zip tapes, until you reach the zip pull, keeping the edge of the foot up against the teeth.

28 Stop the machine, place the needle in the fabric and raise the presser foot.

29 Close the zip, lower the presser foot and carry on stitching to the end of the fabric.

Note:
Don't be tempted to stitch around the bottom of the zip and up the other side. If you do this, it is likely that the zip will appear slightly twisted and the top edges may not meet or lie flat.

30 Move the needle to the left side of the foot and repeat the procedure above again keeping the foot up against the teeth.

Add Your Piping

31 Iron the remaining fabric from the back panel

32 Lay the ironed fabric out on a flat surface.

33 Fold over one corner diagonally to a depth of about 12" so the edges of the fold are at right angles to the edges of the fabric.

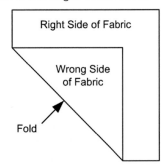

Right Side of Fabric

Wrong Side of Fabric

Fold

34 Lay a quilter's 24" ruler along the folded edge to a depth of 1½".

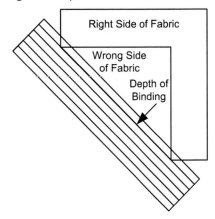

Right Side of Fabric

Wrong Side of Fabric

Depth of Binding

35 Carefully cut along the rule with a rotary cutter.

36 Open out the folded strip and cut in half along its length to form 2 strips of the same width.

37 Continue cutting strips in this manner until you have enough to reach around your cushion cover plus 6" (15cm).

Joining Bias Strips Together

38 To join the bias strips into one long strip, take two strips and lay them right side up as shown in the diagram.

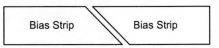

Bias Strip   Bias Strip

39 Now fold one strip over the other as shown below with the points overlapping

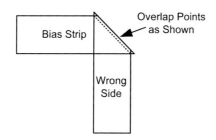

40 Stitch using a ¼" (1cm) seam.

41 Join all your bias strips together on the bias until you have one long strip. Each time you join a strip check to see that all your seam allowances are on the same side.

42 Press seams open.

43 Fold your long bias strip in half lengthways, wrong sides together, and lay the piping cord inside against the fold. If the bias strip is longer than the cord, cut to the same length as the cord.

44 Fit a zipper foot to your sewing machine.

45 Place your folded piping under the machine foot with the piping cord butted up against the edge of the foot and stitch – using a 2.5mm stitch – the full length of the bias strip.

Piping

Attaching the Piping

46 Using a small round disc such as the lid of a box of pins, round off the corners of the front cushion panel using tailor's chalk to mark the line and trim with scissors.

47 Beginning midway on one of the long edges, pin your piping all the way round the right side of the front cushion panel, matching the raw edges together and leaving a tail of 2-3" at each end of the piping.

48 To join the two ends of the binding, unpick a few stitches so you can open out the fabric. Place the ends right side together, so the binding is a snug fit around the cushion panel edge, and stitch so the seam will lie flat.

49 Trim seam allowance to ½" and press open.

50 Trim the piping cord ends so they overlap each other by 1" approx. Cut off 1" approx from one of the three strands of each end of piping and 'knit' the remaining 4 ends together .

51 Fold over the seamed binding and pin in place.

52 With your zipper foot resting lightly against the piping cord (you will press it closer to the piping when stitching the cushion back on) stitch the binding to the cushion front panel.

Assemble Your Cushion

53 Lay your front panel, with attached piping, face up on a flat surface.

54 Round off the corners of the back panel in the same way as the front panel.

55 Open the zip about halfway so you can turn the cushion the right way out after stitching.

56 Lay the back panel face down on top of the front panel

57 Pin edges together all the way round ensuring that the piping stays inside the cushion cover.

58 With the zipper foot fitted, stitch all the way round, keeping the edge of the foot as close as possible to the piping.

59 When you have stitched round once, turn the cushion cover the right way out to check that you have caught in all the edges and stitched close enough to the piping.

60 Now turn it inside out again and work a second line of stitching.

61 Fit a zig-zag foot to your machine and work a line of 4mm wide, 1.5mm length zig-zag stitch all the way round to prevent fraying

62 Turn the cover the right way out, press around the piped edges, avoiding the embroidered image and insert a cushion pad.

Part 7: Using Dissolvable Fabrics

Using free-machine embroidery and dissolvable fabrics to create 3D designs.

Dissolvable Fabrics – Ideas and Inspirations

There is a wide range of dissolvable fabrics on the market today and using these can literally bring a whole new dimension to your sewing.

Dissolvable Fabrics

Dissolvable fabrics can be used to make your own machine stitched lace, adding lacy borders to existing items or, by trapping pieces of fabric between two layers of film, you can even make your own unique fabrics.

Dissolvable fabric is really a glue-based embroidery stabiliser which vanishes when swished in hot or cold water.

Cold Water –Soluble Fabric

This is the most commonly used type of dissolvable fabric. It is made under various brand names by various manufacturers and usually comes in two weights. The standard weight looks and feels a little like cling film. It is easily torn, and I find it better to use a double layer and a ballpoint needle. It is not a good idea to do much dense stitching in any one area as the plastic is liable to come apart. It is better to add stitching to each area in turn and return to any one area that may need a little more.

The extra strong version of cold water soluble fabric looks a little like papery muslin and is much more suitable for dense stitching even when using a single layer.

When all stitching is complete, the piece is placed in a bowl of cold water, swished about to remove any remaining bits and removed. If you wish to remove all the glue, so the piece will be pliable and soft to handle, you can run it under lukewarm water until all the gumminess has gone. If you want to retain a bit of body in your piece, so it can be used in a 3-dimensional piece for example, don't wash out all the residue.

The piece will need to be laid onto kitchen towel to drain and pinned out into its desired shape to dry. If you have a piece of extended polystyrene

left over from packaging, this makes an ideal pinning board. If not, just lay a couple of sheets of kitchen towel or a tea-towel on your ironing board and stab the pins through the paper and into the ironing board.

Hot Water-Soluble Fabric

This product is similar to the cold water version but needs to be dissolved in hot water. Due to the heat involved, there may be some shrinkage, but the effects of this can be lessened by pinning to shape as soon as the piece is removed from the water.

Heat Dissolving Fabric

This method involves pressing the finished piece with a very hot iron to literally burn away the dissolving fabric. It can only be successfully used on good quality machine embroidery threads which are able to withstand the heat of the iron.

The piece must be pressed face down and covered with a cloth to protect the stitched surface. The iron should be moved from place to place until the fabric turns to ash and can be brushed away.

This is not a method I have used and consequently can't recommend. I prefer water to fire and prefer to stick to the water-soluble option.

What Can I Make with Dissolvable Fabrics?

Dissolvable fabrics are great for a wide range of Free-Machine embroidered items. You can stitch out any shape you can think of, dissolve it from its supporting background and then use it to decorate bags, phone and tablet cases, wall hangings, cushions and tablecloths. You can us it to make your own range of Christmas decorations for the tree.

Flowers and Leaves

Flowers, leaves and all sorts of botanical shapes are ideal for free-machine embroidery on dissolvable fabric.

Flowers can be used as bag decorations and leaves could even be turned in to a winter wreath with the addition of a few cinnamon sticks and seed heads.

Christmas Decorations

You can make your own unique range of Christmas decorations using dissolvable fabric. What about some unique ornaments for the tree in the shape of snowflakes, bells, angels, snowmen or Santa and his reindeer. You could even make a standing Christmas angel for the mantelpiece. You could use some metallic threads to add a few sparkly decorations to grown-up Christmas stockings or join in the rather strange craze of wineglass charms.

Adding Decoration to Small Items

Do you have a small bag or phone case that you'd like to jazz up with an embroidered edge? Just sandwich it between two layers of cold water-soluble fabric and put the whole thing in a hoop. Create your own interlocked edging around the item and link it by frequently stitching into the very edge of the case or bag.

Bag and Phone Charms

We carry so many bags, cases and bits of technology around with us these days that is nice to personalise them by adding a few things that reflect what we like. So why not make your own? I've added a project at the end of this section that includes making your own handles and charms for a snazzy evening bag.

Dissolvable Fabrics - Skills and Techniques

Dissolvable fabrics can be used to create many spectacular effects, from bag handle charms to three-dimensional objects.

Using Dissolvable Fabrics

The basic technique of stitching on dissolvable fabrics is very much like stitching onto ordinary fabrics but with two important differences. All the stitching that is done on your piece of hooped, dissolvable fabric must be interlocked, that is all lines of stitches must connect with each other, so, when the fabric is dissolved, the stitched area won't fall to pieces.

Hooping techniques are the same as used for ordinary fabrics – as discussed in Part one of this book – but care must be taken not to tear the fabric when attaching the outer ring of and when pulling it taut in the hoop.

Drawing out Designs.

Once you've decided what you want to embroider using dissolvable fabric, it is a good idea to draw it out first. The fragile nature of the fabric means it is virtually impossible to take out any stitching without tearing and you will end up having to use a new piece. So, using a soft pencil or gel pen, make a sketch of what you are going to embroider on the hooped fabric. It doesn't really matter what you use to draw your design as the lines will disappear with the fabric.

Starting to Stitch

When you start to stitch your drawn design:

1 Outline the shape with straight stitches.

2 Follow this line on the inside of the shape and stitch lots of circles which overlap the outline and each other.

3 Continue stitching, overlapping each circle with the next until the shape is filled. This is your base layer.

4 If more stitching is required, add layers as required. It is not as important to interlock following layers as the base layer and outline will support the further layers.

5 Once you have finished your stitching, the fabric will need to be dissolved in accordance with the manufacturer's instructions and securely pinned out to the final shape and left to dry overnight.

Project – Evening Bag

This little bag is full of interesting and decorative techniques that you will want to practice on lots of other projects.

You Will Need

- ½m (½yd) of organza fabric.
- ½m (½yd) of silky lining in a toning shade.
- ½m (½yd) fusible web.
- Scraps of organza and metallic net in various colours (or anything else sparkly).
- Small ball of Aran (worsted) weight yarn for handles.
- Square of cold water-dissolvable embroidery fabric (stabilizer).
- Embroidery hoop – a small one will be fine.
- Selection of rayon and metallic embroidery threads.
- Baking paper.

Machine Setup

All seam allowances are ½" (1.25cm) unless stated otherwise.

A 2.5mm stitch length is used throughout except for the addition of appliqué images.

A standard zig-zag foot is used throughout unless otherwise stated.

To Make Your Bag

Cut Your Pattern Pieces

1 From the organza, cut 4 x 10" squares.

2 From the lining, cut 2 x 9" squares.

3 From the fusible web, cut 2 x 10" squares.

Make the Front and Back Panels

4 Place a large sheet of baking paper onto your ironing board and on top place two of the organza squares, side by side, followed by the one square of fusible web on each, glue side downwards.

> **Note:**
> If you are using a double sided fusible web, remove one of the paper backings before placing the square onto the organza.

5 Press, using a medium iron until the fusible web is secured.

6 Peel off the backing.

7 Cut a variety of small pieces from the organza and metallic net scraps and scatter these randomly over each of the organza squares (glue side). Try and completely cover the fusible web.

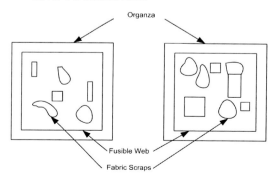

8   Place the two remaining organza squares on top of the scraps and cover with another sheet of baking paper.

9   Press firmly with a medium to hot iron until the organza sandwich pieces are secure. These pieces will form the front and back of your bag.

10 Using a variety of matching and contrasting embroidery threads and a selection of your machine's decorative stitches, sew lines of stitching all over the front and back pieces of your bag, swinging the fabric gently from side to side as you stitch to form wavy lines.

11 When you are satisfied with your stitching, place your two organza sandwich pieces on the cutting board and trim to 9" square.

12 Place the two organza pieces right sides together and sew a ½" seam round three sides.

13 Trim the seams and corners and turn inside out.

Add a Luxurious Lining

14 Take the two 9" square pieces of lining fabric and, with wrong sides together, sew a ½" seam down two opposite sides, leaving the top and bottom edges open.

15 Slide your bag into the lining with the right sides together and the raw top edges together. Pin the top edges all round and stitch, leaving ½" seam allowance.

16 Pull the lining up over the bag.

17 Turn in ½" on the bottom raw edge of the lining and press. Stitch close to the folded edge.

18 Push the lining down into the bag.

Create Some Funky Handles

19 Decide how long you want your bag handles to be (including the decorated pieces hanging down each side) and multiply this measurement by 10.

20 Set your machine for free-arm embroidery by referring to your machine instruction book. Remove the presser foot.

21 Using the measurement taken in step 19, cut two lengths of Aran-weight yarn, of this length, and knot them together at one end.

22 Set your sewing machine to the widest zig-zag stitch setting, drop the presser foot handle (this is important for engaging the tension), and, holding the knotted ends of the yarn behind the needle and the remaining yarn in front (ensuring your hands are completely clear of the needle bed at all times) stitch over the two strands of yarn, twisting them together slightly as you go. Try to keep the speed of the machine fairly constant. The depth of colour depends on how fast you move the yarns through the needle. As your feed dogs are down you are free to move as fast or slow as you wish and can even go back and forwards to form the occasional thread 'bobble'.

23 When you reach the end of your yarn 'cord', thread your machine with a different colour and go over the whole thing again. This can be repeated until you achieve the depth of colour you want.

Add Some Free-Embroidered Decorations

24 Take a small sheet of dissolvable machine embroidery fabric and secure in an embroidery hoop.

25 Set your machine for straight stitch and attach a darning foot if you have one.

26 Lightly draw a few small stars or flowers on your fabric and position the hoop under the needle.

27 Keeping the machine running at a reasonably fast and constant speed, outline the first of your shapes twice.

28 To fill in your shape, rotate the hoop gently while sewing so you achieve small loops which intersect the outline of the shape and

each other.(If the stitching is not joined together, the whole thing will fall apart when you dissolve the backing fabric).

29 Continue in this way until you have 16 shapes (one for each end of your eight handles).

30 Remove the fabric from the hoop and immerse in about 2" of warm water. When the fabric is dissolved, lift out each shape and pin out on either an ironing board or cork tile. Leave to dry.

31 In the meantime, cut your yarn 'cord' into eight handles of the original bag handle measurement.

32 Satin stitch a shape to each end of each handle.

33 Gather the completed handles into two bundles of four. Mark the handle position on the front and back of your bag – 2" from each side seam.

34 Ensuring that each of the handles lie flat along their length, pin each end in position on the bag and sew over in straight stitch three or four times.

35 Organise a night off to show off your bag!

Part 8: What Next?

Here are some other books and inspirations you might like to look at.

More from Time4me Workshops

You can find more tips, techniques, videos and books at Margo Price's website.

Time4me-Workshops Website

The aim of my website is to promote traditional crafts by passing on knowledge, skills and experience to those who would like to learn about, or perhaps already enjoy, sewing.

In these pages you will find practical advice that will make your sewing projects easier and more enjoyable. You'll find advice on choosing and using wadding, getting started in dressmaking and top tips on appliqué.

Why not take a look at my videos on how to use men's shirts to make a traditional quilt? Or if cushion making is more your thing, there are a series of six videos showing you all you need to know.

To find out more, visit Margo Price's website at:

time4me-workshops.co.uk

How to Make a Living from Crafts

Using the craft of sewing as an example, this book will also provide essential reading for other craftsmen such as musicians, photographers, jewellery makers, card makers, knitters, woodworkers, gardeners, watercolour painters, clay modellers, mosaic artists, and many more.

This online e-book (soon also to be available in other formats) is suited to intermediate and advanced crafters who are producing work good enough to sell or who may be selling their wares already but are struggling to make a living. It also explains the benefits of branching out and teaching your skill to others and shows you how to set up and run your workshops.

To purchase this book, or find out more, visit Margo Price's website at:

time4me-workshops.co.uk

Or visit the Kindle Store at www.amazon.co.uk or www.amazon.com

How to Sew With Confidence

Do you want to make the designs you see in sewing magazines or on the web? Has your sewing machine been lurking in the under stairs cupboard since you bought it? Do you lack the confidence to take control of your sewing machine?

This book provides the perfect jargon-free starter guide for those who would love to master their sewing machine. With a collection of simple, but stylish, sewing projects and a detailed reference section of basic techniques, this book guides you, step-by-step, through the basics of machine sewing.

This online e-book (soon also to be available in other formats) is suited to beginners and those who want to be more confident in their sewing.

To purchase this book, or find out more, visit Margo Price's website at:

time4me-workshops.co.uk

Or visit the Kindle Store at www.amazon.co.uk or www.amazon.com

Other Books You May Like

This book was written to give you a flavour of just what is possible with free-machine embroidery. If you've enjoyed it and would like to pursue any aspect of this fascinating craft further, here are a few books you might like to read.

Freestyle Machine Embroidery: Techniques and Inspirations for Fiber Art
by Carol Shinn

Free-Motion Quilting: Choose and Use Quilting Designs for Modern Quilts
by Angela Walters

Beginner's Guide to Machine Embroidered Landscapes
by Alison Holt

They are all available on Amazon but not all on Kindle.

43747851R00043

Made in the USA
San Bernardino, CA
26 December 2016